Where was God on September 11?

John Blanchard

EVANGELICAL PRESS

EVANGELICAL PRESS
Faverdale North Industrial Estate, Darlington, DL3 0PH, England

Evangelical Press USA
P. O. Box 84, Auburn, MA 01501, USA

e-mail: sales@evangelicalpress.org

web: http://www.evangelicalpress.org

First published January 2002
Second impression February 2002
Third impression March 2002
Fourth impression April 2002
Fifth impression May 2002
Sixth impression July 2002

British Library Cataloguing in Publication Data available

ISBN 0 85234 508 9

Printed and bound in Great Britain by Bailes the Printer, Houghton-le-Spring, Tyne & Wear

Where was God on September 11?

Few adults alive at the time will ever forget where they were when they heard that United States President John F. Kennedy had been assassinated in Dallas, Texas, on 22 November 1963. Nearly thirty-eight years later another event in the United States was to leave an even more traumatic impression.

For thirty years the twin towers of the World Trade Centre dominated the skyline of Manhattan, the business heart of New York City. If we include the 347-foot radio mast on top of the north tower, it was the tallest building in the world. The centre's 110 storeys provided twelve million square feet of space serviced by 103 elevators, sixteen miles of staircases, 12,000 miles of electric cable and 49,000 tons of air-conditioning equipment. On the morning of 11 September 2001 thousands of people streamed into the twin towers to begin work. It seemed a day like any other day, but some 300 miles to the north-east co-ordinated teams of religious fanatics were preparing to shatter that illusion.

In a meticulously planned operation, they hijacked two commercial airlines on scheduled flights from Boston to Los Angeles. Brutally slitting the throats of passengers or crew members who tried to stop them, they re-routed the Boeing 767s to New York, flew in over Manhattan and aimed the aircraft at the World Trade Centre like guided missiles.

At 8.45 on that beautiful September morning, American Airlines Flight 11, with ninety-two people on board, tore into the north tower, its 20,000 gallons of aviation fuel igniting a blaze that reached an estimated temperature of 2,000 degrees Fahrenheit. About twenty minutes later — now covered by live television — United Airlines Flight 175, carrying sixty-five people, buried itself in the south tower, with the same catastrophic results.

Gaping holes appeared on the upper levels of the towers, releasing massive balls of fire and clouds of dense black smoke that smothered the city. Desks, chairs, filing cabinets and computer equipment, together with human bodies and body parts, were blown or sucked out of the building and rained down on the earth 'like ticker tape' on to the streets below. Terrified workers smashed windows and threw themselves out. One witness told of seeing at least fourteen people floating down like rag dolls. A man and a woman held hands as they hurtled to their deaths.

Less than an hour after it had been hit, the south tower crumpled to the ground in a cloud of metal, concrete and glass, setting off a huge mushroom cloud of yellow dust. About thirty minutes later the north tower collapsed, adding to a dust cloud so massive and dense that it blotted out the sun.

In what the *Economist* called 'this unspeakable crime', one of the world's mightiest buildings had been reduced to two jagged stumps looking for all the world like the ruins of some ancient cathedral jutting out from a gigantic mountain of smouldering rubble which had become a hideous headstone over the bodies of nearly 3,000 men, women and children who had been in or near the building when the terrorists struck. The event was so appalling that it virtually overshadowed the news that a third hijacked airliner had been steered into the Pentagon in Washington, DC., killing nearly 200 people, and that a fourth had crashed near Pittsburgh, Pennsylvania, with the loss of forty-five lives. It was the bloodiest day in the nation's history since its Civil War, which ended in 1865, and the most murderous and devastating terrorist attack the world had ever known.

In Britain, *The Times* called it 'a tragedy that stretched human powers of understanding to breaking point'. The twin towers had been designed to represent man's belief in humanity, but one newspaper said that, with the terrorists' attack, 'The landscape of America's belief has been destroyed. *The Times'* leading article was headed, 'The day that changed the modern world,' while a *Daily Mail* columnist wrote, 'History will never be the same again.'

Within hours, the media were awash with questions. How could such a thing possibly happen? Why did the United States' Intelligence services not anticipate an event that must have taken many months of planning? Who was responsible for masterminding the attack? What could — or should — be done to punish them and to prevent such a thing ever happening again?

Atheists and agnostics — and millions of people who were neither — had another, more fundamental question, and a *Daily Telegraph* reader supplied it: 'How can anyone argue that this is what his God believes to be appropriate behaviour?' Within days, in several different settings, I was challenged with a fine-tuned version of the same question: 'Where was God when the terrorists attacked America?' The question is inescapable and the argument behind it goes back thousands of years. It can be summed up like this:

1. If God were all-powerful he could prevent evil and suffering.
2. If he were all-loving, he would want to prevent them.
3. Evil and suffering exist.
4. God is therefore impotent, loveless or non-existent.

The philosopher Alvin Plantinga calls this 'the only argument against God that deserves to be taken seriously', and most people who deny or doubt the existence of God do so along these lines. You may be one of them.

'Ragged edges'

The fundamental fact that triggers off the whole argument is undeniable: evil and suffering are universal facts of life, brutally confirming that we live in what someone has called 'a world with ragged edges'.

Natural disasters

Earthquakes, volcanoes, floods, hurricanes, tidal waves, fires and other natural disasters have killed or injured millions of people, often wiping out huge numbers within a few hours. Over one million died when China's Hwang-ho river burst its banks in 1887. Some 200,000 perished in an earthquake in the same country's Kansu province in 1920, and 12,000 were drowned and millions made homeless when Hurricane Mitch, dubbed 'the storm of the century', hit Central America in 1998. How can an all-powerful God allow his creation to get out of control in this way?

Accidents

On 14 April 1912 the British liner *Titanic*, then the largest movable object ever made by man, and said to be so well built that 'God himself couldn't sink this ship', struck an iceberg in the North Atlantic on her maiden voyage and sank with the loss of some 1,500 lives.

On 21 October 1966 a slag-heap loosened by persistent rain slithered into the junior school in the Welsh village of Aberfan and smothered to death five teachers and 109 children.

On 26 April 1986 a nuclear reactor in the Ukrainian town of Chernobyl was ripped apart by two explosions which may yet cause up to 300,000 deaths and the effects of which could take up to 200 years to remove.

These three tragedies represent countless others: aeroplanes crash; trains are derailed; road vehicles collide; ships are lost at sea; buildings collapse; bridges give way; trees fall; machinery malfunctions. There are times when the whole world seems like a vast Accident and Emergency

Unit, and every day adds to the millions accidentally killed or injured. Is a loving, caring God presiding over this mayhem?

Built-in hazards

Our planet can supply all our basic needs, but it is also teeming with things that can wipe us out, from poisonous vegetation to killer sharks, to say nothing of countless bacteria and viruses capable of disfiguring, dismembering or destroying us. Even the air we breathe is sometimes contaminated with life-threatening agents of one kind or another. Has God deliberately put all these hazards in place?

Human conflict

It has been estimated that in the last 4,000 years there have been less than 300 without a major war. The twentieth century was expected to be one of unparalleled peace and prosperity, but in 1967 Britain's Secretary of Defence called it 'the most violent century in history'. He was right. Thirty million people were killed in World War I, while the figures for World War II are so vast that they have never been accurately computed. Countless others were ruthlessly put to death during the rise of Marxist-Leninist Communism in Russia and Eastern Europe. At one point, opponents of Mao Tse-tung's Communist Revolution in China were being exterminated at the rate of 22,000 a month. Pol Pot slaughtered over 1,500,000 Cambodians in less than two years. In the six weeks from 7 April 1994 over 500,000 Rwandans were massacred in the savage civil war between Hutus and Tutsis. Could a loving God allow such wholesale carnage?

The ravages of time

As if these dangers and disasters were not enough, we are all fighting a losing battle against physical, mental and psychological deterioration,

and even in an age of organ transplants, microsurgery, genetic manipu-
lation and 'wonder drugs', nobody can buck the trend. When business
tycoon Sumner Redstone, cited in *Forbes* magazine as America's eight-
eenth richest man, told the *Daily Telegraph* in July 2001, 'Death is not on
my agenda,' he was toying with the truth. Living is the process of dying,
and regular exercise, disciplined eating, fitness programmes and the best
of medical attention can only delay the inevitable, which will come to
over 260,000 people today. Is this miserable picture being painted by a
loving God who is said in the Bible to do 'whatever pleases him'? (Psalm
115:3).

God's tombstone?

These are some of atheism's strongest arguments, but for over sixty years
one event has been used more than any other to challenge the idea of an
all-powerful, all-loving God — the Holocaust.

When the German dictator Adolf Hitler set about building the Third
Reich his plans included the establishment of an Aryan 'super-race'. To
achieve this, he decided to get rid of all who were unlikely to make any
worthwhile contribution to a world free from human weakness, including
what he called 'the stupid and degrading fallacies of conscience and
morality'. The physically frail and mentally unstable were obvious candi-
dates for elimination, but his main targets were the Jews (Hitler called
them 'human bacteria') and by the end of the war six million of them —
one-third of the world's entire Jewish population — had been exterminated. The impact on people's thinking has been such that one author
wrote, 'The case against the existence of God can be summed up in two
words: the Holocaust.'

It certainly destroyed the faith of many. The Jewish author Elie Wiesel
survived the concentration camp at Birkenau, and in his powerful book
Night he describes some of its horrors — babies pitchforked as if they

were bales of straw, children watching other children being hanged, and his mother and other members of his own family thrown into a huge furnace fuelled by human bodies. During one of the hanging sessions, Wiesel heard someone groan, 'Where is God? Where is he? Where can he be now?' When it was all over, Wiesel's own reply was that Birkenau 'murdered my God and my soul and turned my dreams to dust'.

The American lawyer Edward Tabash comes from five unbroken generations of orthodox Jewish rabbis, but the Holocaust claimed the lives of two of his own family members and turned him into a passionate atheist prepared to challenge God head-on. In a debate in California he said, 'If the God of the Bible actually exists, I want to sue him for negligence, for being asleep at the wheel of the universe when my grandfather and uncle were gassed to death in Auschwitz.'

Other atheists would agree, and point to one particular reason for doing so: as all Jews worthy of the name believe not merely that God is a living reality, but that they are his chosen people, where was their God when they were being systematically exterminated? What was he doing for the three years during which Jewish men, women and children were being gassed twenty-fours a day in the extermination camps at Auschwitz, Belsen, Dachau and elsewhere? Where was God when Nazi prison guards threw babies and small children into gutters of boiling human fat rather than waste time gassing them? Where was God when the remains of the slaughtered were scavenged — hair cut off to make comfortable cushions for the murderers, tattooed skin peeled off and dried out to make lampshades, and gold tooth fillings pulled out and turned into jewellery? After wrestling with the issue of the Holocaust, the Jewish author Richard Rubenstein wrote, 'We stand in a cold, silent, unfeeling cosmos, unaided by any power beyond our own resources. After Auschwitz, what else can a Jew say about God?'

You may agree — but one Auschwitz survivor came to a very different conclusion. Quoted in *The Times*, he said that he never once questioned God's action (or apparent inaction) while he was an inmate: 'It never occurred to me to associate the calamity we were experiencing with God — to blame him or believe in him less, or cease believing in him at all because he didn't come to our aid. God doesn't owe us that, or anything. We owe our lives to him. If someone believes that God is responsible for the death of six million because he doesn't somehow do something to save them, he's got his thinking reversed.'

This Holocaust survivor is neither a fake nor a freak. He speaks from the heart for countless others who would say that their experience of suffering has strengthened rather than weakened their faith in God and given them a coherent insight into evil and its consequences. Before we examine why they can do this, I have some tough questions to ask those who see the Holocaust as God's tombstone, an obscene testimony to the fact that the idea of a loving Creator being in control of the universe is dead and buried.

What problem?

The Holocaust obviously raises huge questions for people who believe in God, *but why should it cause any problem for atheists?* If the British philosopher Bertrand Russell was right to dismiss man as 'a curious accident in a backwater', why should it matter in the least whether lives are ended slowly or suddenly, peacefully or painfully? If an atheist like the Oxford professor Peter Atkins is right in calling mankind 'just a bit of slime on a planet', why should we be remotely concerned at the systematic slaughter of six million Jews? Do we get traumatized when we see slime trodden on or shovelled down a drain?

The British anthropologist Sir Arthur Keith says that Hitler 'consciously sought to make the practices of Germany conform to the theory of atheistic evolution'. As all atheists are evolutionists, this is highly embarrassing for them, as evolution says that humankind is simply the result of countless chemical and biological accidents. If this is true, how can human beings have any personal value, and why should we turn a hair if any regime disposes of them by the million? The modern American author Henry Morris writes, 'In the biological theory of Darwin, Hitler found his most powerful weapon against human values,' while an Auschwitz survivor says that its gas chambers 'were the ultimate consequence of the theory that man is nothing but the product of heredity and environment'.

Why should the Holocaust raise any *ethical* problems for the atheist? In a godless universe, what one 'animal' does to another 'animal' is morally irrelevant — making it just as easy to commend the Holocaust as to condemn it. Although it caused appalling physical, mental and emotional pain and suffering, *atheism has no way of declaring it to be radically wrong*, as in the absence of absolute, transcendent ethics the word 'wrong' is meaningless. If we live in a world in which everything can be explained by physics, chemistry and biology, things we call 'good' and 'evil' are just impersonal, valueless data with no explanation. If there is no God, there is no universal moral law, and if there is no such law, *nothing* is essentially good or evil. An entrenched atheist like the Oxford zoologist Richard Dawkins concedes this without blinking and says that we live in a universe in which there is 'no design, no purpose, *no evil and no good*, nothing but blind, pitiless indifference'. Can you accept this, and brush aside the Holocaust as a meaningless event in a meaningless world?

Some people see moral values as a social contract aimed at producing what is usually called 'the greatest good of the greatest number', but Hitler would have signed up to that idea in a heartbeat! After all, he justified the extermination of Jews, gypsies, the mentally unstable and others in the long-term interests of a superior race that would eventually dominate the world.

These are tricky areas for the atheist because, as the modern thinker Ravi Zacharias points out, the Holocaust was 'the logical outworking of the demise of God'. Although Hitler was raised in the Roman Catholic Church and kept his formal ties with the church for his own political ends, he abandoned any pretence of faith at an early age. He described himself

as 'a total pagan', and called Christianity 'the hardest blow that ever
struck humanity'. Any honest atheist would admit that he does not have
answers to the questions raised by the Holocaust, but an honest *and
consistent* atheist should realize that *he has no reason or basis to raise
them in the first place.* Logically, evil and suffering are problems only to
people who believe in God.

The other side of the coin

Another flaw in the atheist's case is that logically speaking he has problems not merely with the existence of evil, but with the existence of *good*.
In a universe that can be explained solely in terms of physics, chemistry
and biology, 'good' becomes as meaningless as 'evil'. If you are an atheist, how do you explain goodness, love, kindness, generosity or sym-
pathy? Atheists are clearly *capable* of all of these, but if human beings are
just collections of bones, blood and tissue, what do these things *mean*
and why is there any virtue in them? (Come to think of it, what does
'virtue' mean?) When Richard Dawkins admits that 'Universal love and
the welfare of the species as a whole simply do not make evolutionary
sense,' he is confirming that there is no way to arrive at personal morality
from an impersonal universe. How can we jump from atoms to ethics
and from molecules to morality? If we are nothing but genetically programmed machines, how can we condemn anything as being 'evil', or
commend anything as being 'good'? Why should we be concerned over
issues of justice or fairness, or feel any obligation to treat others with
dignity or respect?

People sometimes respond to tragedy by asking, 'How can there be a
just God?' but the question is logically flawed. How do these people get
the idea of things being just or unjust? Without a God of absolute justice,
words like 'just' and 'unjust' have no moral content but are matters of
personal opinion at best and meaningless at worst. Far from moral problems ruling out the existence of God, our sense of things being right or

wrong, fair or unfair, just or unjust provides a strong clue that there is some transcendent standard that affects us all. As the philosopher Alvin Plantinga points out, atheists are coming to realize this: 'Now, as opposed to 20-25 years ago, most [atheists] have conceded that in fact there isn't any inconsistency between the existence of an omnipotent, omniscient and wholly good God and the existence of the evil the world contains.' Had you grasped that the existence of evil points *towards* the existence of God, not away from it?

Facing facts

There is no way in which the person who believes in the God revealed in the Bible can evade the issue of evil and suffering, but before we look at what the Bible says on the subject we need to nail down some basic facts.

- Although our planet provides enough food to feed all six billion of us, millions die of starvation every year because of our exploitation or mismanagement of the earth's resources and the vicious policies of dictatorial regimes, while the selfish pollution of the atmosphere results in agony and death for many others. Can we blame God for this?
- Suffering is often caused by human error or incompetence. The owners of the *Titanic* reduced the recommended number of lifeboats to avoid the boat deck looking cluttered. The Aberfan enquiry pinpointed the 'bungling ineptitude' of those who built the slag-heap over a stream. The International Atomic Enquiry Agency blamed 'defective safety culture' for the Chernobyl disaster. Even if we ignore the many millions who have been killed or wounded in military conflict and in acts of personal violence, these examples are sufficient to show that man himself is directly responsible for a great deal of human suffering. How can we put God in the dock?

- A great deal of human suffering is self-inflicted. Smokers who ignore health warnings and are crippled by lung cancer or heart disease, heavy drinkers who suffer from cirrhosis of the liver, drug addicts and those dying of AIDS after indiscriminate sex are obvious examples. So are gluttons whose health collapses, workaholics who drive themselves to physical or mental breakdowns, and the countless people who suffer from serious illness as a direct result of suppressed hatred, anger, bitterness and envy. Can we seriously blame God for their behaviour?

The link between wrongdoing and its consequences is so clear that we need to get personal here. Ravi Zacharias tells of a discussion he and some friends had with one of America's biggest construction tycoons who wanted to know why God was silent when there was so much evil in the world. At one point someone asked him, 'Since evil seems to trouble you so much, I would be curious to know what you have done about the evil you see within you.' There was what Zacharias called 'a red-faced silence'. How would you have responded? Are you ruthlessly doing everything you can to root out from your life whatever you sense to be less than perfect?

The blurred reflection

When we turn to the Bible, the first thing we notice is that far from giving slick and easy answers to the questions raised by evil and suffering, it confirms that we all have to reckon with 'the secret power of lawlessness' (2 Thessalonians 2:7). At first glance, this may seem to be evading the issue, but there is no logical basis for assuming that God owes us a detailed explanation for everything that goes on in the world — and leaving us with questions is not the same as leaving us in the dark. The Bible confirms that, in this life, 'We see but a poor reflection as in a mirror' (1 Corinthians 13:12). Why should this surprise us, or make us decide that God is non-existent? How could we know all the answers unless we had total knowledge of everything? To say that unless we see the whole picture there *is* no picture is not intelligence but arrogance.

In Paul's day a mirror would have been made from burnished metal, giving a somewhat blurred image; but it would still have given some indication of what it was reflecting. On the issue of evil and suffering, even the strongest believer in God has to admit that there are enigmas, grey areas and unanswered questions. Yet to say that something is mysterious is not to say that we can know nothing about it, and we can now turn to look at some of the Bible's teaching on the subject. There is only one place to begin.

The stained planet

An article in *The Times* once asked, 'What's wrong with the world?' In the correspondence that followed, the shortest letter was by far the best:

> In response to your question, 'What's wrong with the world?' —
> I am.
>   Yours faithfully,
>   G. K. Chesterton.

The well-known British author's confession rings a bell; when looking for somebody to blame for evil and suffering, nobody is in a position to point an accusing finger at God.

The Bible says that when God created the world it was without blemish of any kind, reflecting his own perfect nature: 'God saw all that he had made, and it was very good' (Genesis 1:31). Included in this perfect world was humanity, distinct from all the rest of creation in being made 'in the image of God' (Genesis 1:27), a phrase that tells us at least three things about man.

1. He was created as a *personal* being, capable of a living relationship with his Creator and with his fellow human beings.

2. He was created as a *moral* being, his conscience making him aware by nature of the difference between right and wrong.

3. He was created as a *rational* being, able not merely to think, draw conclusions and make sensible decisions, but specifically to make moral choices. Although moral perfection was stamped upon him at his creation, he was not a robot, programmed to do whatever God dictated. Instead, he had the ability to obey God and the freedom to disobey him.

This state of perfection went on for some time, but at some point a created angel or spirit called Satan, who had rebelled against God's authority, persuaded Adam and his wife Eve to disbelieve God and disobey his clear directions. The moment they did so, 'Sin entered the world' (Romans 5:12) — with catastrophic results.

- Man's relationship with God, which had depended on unqualified obedience to his perfect will, was shattered. Man retained his spiritual nature, but lost his spiritual life. He remained a person, but forfeited dynamic union with his Maker.
- He lost his innocence and his moral free will, his very nature becoming infected with godless ideas, attitudes and affections.
- His own personality was wrecked. He lost his self-esteem and for the first time knew what it was to be guilty, alienated, ashamed, anxious and afraid.
- His inter-personal relationships were poisoned by suspicion, dishonesty, mistrust and the need to justify himself.
- His body became subject to decay, disease and death, things that were never built into man's original make-up.

Two things bring the history of human rebellion right up to date. Adam sinned as the representative head of the entire human race and, because humanity is an integrated whole, he took the entire species with him: 'Sin entered the world through one man, and death through sin, and in this way death came to all men, because all sinned' (Romans 5:12). Tied in to this is the fact that Adam began to father children *after* his fall into sin and that he did so 'in his own likeness, in his own image' (Genesis 5:3). Like poison dumped at the source of a river, Adam's polluted and depraved nature has been passed on to every succeeding generation, and all of humanity is caught up in its flow. You and I did not begin life in a state of moral neutrality, but with sinful tendencies and desires waiting to express themselves in words, thoughts and actions. Does your own experience not confirm this?

Rebellion against a God of infinite goodness, holiness and truth is infinitely evil, and the consequences were so far-reaching that the entire cosmos was dislocated, leaving the whole creation 'groaning as in the pains of childbirth right up to the present time' (Romans 8:22). The world as we now see it is not in its original condition, but is radically ruined by sin, and we live on what someone has called 'a stained planet'. Earthquakes, volcanoes, floods and hurricanes were unknown before sin entered the world, and the suffering and death they cause are due to what the British author Stuart Olyott calls 'contempt for God', man's rebellion against his Maker's authority.

The big question here is why God should have taken such an obvious risk in giving man moral freedom in the first place. Whatever the answer might be, not even an all-powerful God could give man freedom and at the same time guarantee that he would use it wisely. A person who is free and yet not free is a contradiction in terms; not even God could bestow and withhold freedom at one and the same time. Yet to deny that God could possibly have arranged things the way he did is going too far, as the Bible says that his wisdom and love are infinite and that 'His way is perfect' (Psalm 18:30).

Can we possibly prove that God was wrong to give man freedom of moral choice? Would creating robots have been wiser? How can we know God's reasons and purposes unless we know everything he knows? In his

book *How Long, O Lord?*, the American author Don Carson writes that
God's way of working 'defies our attempt to tame it by reason', then
adds, 'I do not mean it is illogical; I mean that we do not know enough to
be able to unpack it and domesticate it.' As finite, fallen creatures we
need to swallow our pride and accept that God's ways are beyond our
finite understanding. Refusing to do this, and claiming that the existence
of evil rules out our creation by a wise and loving God, is irrational,
illogical and unbiblical.

An interfering God?

But would an all-powerful, all-loving God not intervene to prevent evil
and the suffering it causes? That question is best answered by asking
others.

What kind of God would do this whenever we wanted him to? In the
debate mentioned earlier, Edward Tabash called God a 'moral monster'
and issued this challenge: 'If you are listening, and you are really there,
show yourself right now... Do a colossal miracle... Show me something
more than ancient hearsay to prove your existence.' When nothing happened, Tabash claimed to have proved his case — but he missed the
point that a God who allowed himself to be ordered around in this way
would be surrendering the very qualities that make him God. The kind of
God who jumps whenever anybody (atheist or otherwise) shouts, 'Jump!'
may exist in fairy tales but not in the real world.

Do we really want God to prevent things happening (or cause other
things to happen) by manipulating the laws of physics in such a way that
we would never know from one moment to another which were working
and which had been suspended? If God tweaked the laws of nature bil-
lions of times a day merely to ensure everybody's safety, comfort or suc-
cess, science would be impossible and, as Francis Bridger says in his

book *Why Can't I Have Faith?*, 'We should be reduced to such a state of physical, social and psychological instability that life would fall apart, paradoxically bringing even more suffering in its train.'

Turning to moral issues, at what level should God intervene? We might say that he should not have allowed the worst offenders — the Hitlers, Pol Pots and Mao Tse-tungs of this world — to do what they did. But what about the next level — say, thugs, sadists, rapists, child abusers and drug pushers — should God step in and stop them? If he did so, another 'layer' of offenders would become the worst — say, drunk drivers, shop-lifters, burglars and the like. If we argued like this we would soon get to the point at which we would be demanding that God should intervene to prevent *all* evil. Would you settle for that, even if it meant having your own thoughts, words and actions controlled by a cosmic puppet-master, robbing you of all freedom and responsibility?

This kind of God would also need to control thoughts and actions that were the *indirect* causes of suffering. After my weekly game of golf I drive to pick up my wife from another appointment. Imagine that I am delayed by those playing in front of me, then find that I am running behind schedule. Dashing out of the clubhouse to the car park, I accidentally knock over a lady member who hits her head so violently on a concrete kerb that she sustains irreparable brain damage. How should God have intervened to prevent subsequent years of suffering? By causing the players in front of me to play better or faster? By making me choose an earlier starting time? By shortening the time it took me to shower and change after the game? By steering the lady into the clubhouse through a different door? Would you honestly accept the idea of a God who manipulated things in this way, squeezing out every atom of your independence or choice?

Suggesting that God should intervene to prevent all evil and suffering sounds reasonable in theory, but when we think it through it raises more problems than it solves. The Bible points us in a very different direction.

A case history

The Bible's fullest treatment of the issue of evil and suffering is the story of a man called Job, who lived over 3,000 years ago. Rated 'the greatest man among all the people of the East' (Job 1:3), he was seriously wealthy and the father of seven sons and three daughters. What is more, he was 'blameless and upright; he feared God and shunned evil' (Job 1:1). He seemed to have everything going for him, but in one terrible day he lost over 11,000 animals, many of his servants were killed and all his ten children died when a tornado struck the house in which they were holding a party (see Job 1:13-19). Yet after being hit by this personal holocaust, Job 'fell to the ground in worship' and said:

> Naked I came from my mother's womb,
>   and naked I shall depart.
> The LORD gave and the LORD has taken away;
>   may the name of the LORD be praised
>
>   (Job 1:20-21).

This was a stupendous declaration of faith in the sovereignty of God, but it did nothing to stop Job's suffering. His own health began to deteriorate; he was covered with boils, his skin began to peel off, his eyes grew weak, his teeth began to rot and he was hit by a combination of fever, insomnia and depression. Those nearest to him turned the screw and his wife was so sure things were hopeless that she indirectly challenged him to commit suicide: 'Curse God and die!' (Job 2:9). An inner circle of friends began by being sympathetic, but soon changed their tune and told Job that his great suffering must be punishment for great sin, one of them even suggesting that Job was probably getting off lightly.

From then on, Job rode an emotional roller-coaster. At one point he wished he had been stillborn: 'Why did I not perish at birth?' (Job 3:11), while at other times he looked forward to an infinitely fuller life after death and the prospect of spending eternity in God's presence: 'I know that my Redeemer lives... I myself will see him with my own eyes' (Job 19:25). He questioned God's justice in allowing the ungodly to 'spend their years in prosperity and go down to the grave in peace' (Job 21:13), while he was 'reduced to dust and ashes' (Job 30:19). There were periods when he felt that God was either distant or deaf, with no concern for his pain and no inclination to answer his prayers. Throughout this time, his friends kept up such a barrage of questions, advice and accusations that Job complained, 'Will your long-winded speeches never end?' (Job 16:3). Then came the decisive turning-point of the whole story — God spoke directly to Job.

God's response to Job's agonizing questions forms the Bible's fullest treatment of the issue of evil and suffering — yet it never mentions either! Instead of giving Job a neatly packaged explanation, God took a very different line. Often in the form of questions, Job was reminded of the way in which the natural world pointed to God's overwhelming greatness and power in contrast to man's dependence and weakness:

Where were you when I laid the earth's foundation?

(Job 38:4).

Have you ever given orders to the morning
    or shown the dawn its place?

(Job 38:12).

Can you bind the beautiful Pleiades?
    Can you loose the cords of Orion?

(Job 38:31).

Do you send the lightning bolts on their way?

(Job 38:35).

Can you set up God's dominion over the earth?

(Job 38:33).

Do you have an arm like God's?

(Job 40:9).

The closest God came to answering Job's questions directly was to ask some of his own:

Will the one who contends with the Almighty correct him? …
Would you discredit my justice?
Would you condemn me to justify yourself?

(Job 40:1,8).

God told him nothing about the cause of pain and suffering, but focused instead on man's response. The torrent of words poured out by his friends had done nothing to bring Job clarity, comfort or courage — they had been 'words without knowledge' (Job 38:2) — but now he was able to see things in their right perspective

- God was in absolute control of the universe, and nothing could frustrate his eternal purposes: 'I know that you can do all things; no plan of yours can be thwarted' (Job 42:1).
- He was in no position to argue with God or to question his dealings with him: 'I am unworthy — how can I reply to you?' (Job 40:4).
- He was not in possession of all the facts: 'Surely I spoke of things I did not understand, things too wonderful for me to know' (Job 42:3).
- A living relationship with God was infinitely better than religious feelings or ideas: 'My ears had heard of you but now my eyes have seen you' (Job 42:5).

- He should confess that he had been wrong to question God's power, justice and love and should humbly commit himself to him: 'I despise myself and repent in dust and ashes' (Job 42:6).

There are important principles here. Job did not get a line-by-line answer to his questions, but he learned to trust God in the dark. This was not giving in to fate but, as the Irish preacher Herbert Carson movingly puts it, responding 'like a child in the darkness gripped in his father's arms'. God does not spell out to us why he allowed sin to enter the universe but, without telling us how this works out in practice, assures us that he is in control of even the worst of its effects.

Job's story tells us that *it is less important to know all the answers than to know and trust the one who does.* Laying hold on this alone can be a liberating experience. Some years ago my wife was being crushed by life-threatening clinical depression. Her faith had virtually evaporated and there seemed to be no relief in sight. Then, twice in one week, people wrote to her in almost identical words, the gist of their messages being that God was under no obligation to explain anything that he caused or allowed to come into our lives. This did not give us cut-and-dried answers to all our questions, but within a day or so the suffocating cloud had lifted and Joyce emerged with her faith renewed and deepened.

God's megaphone

In his well-known book *The Problem of Pain,* C. S. Lewis wrote, 'God whispers to us in our pleasures, speaks in our conscience, but shouts in our pains; it is his megaphone to rouse a deaf world.' Lewis was right. Life's pleasant experiences have often been seen as tokens of God's goodness, while sudden stabs of conscience have frequently brought a sense of moral responsibility. But how does God 'shout in our pains'? In many ways. The Bible tells us that God uses suffering to underline our physical frailty, to remind us that we are not immune from the consequences of sin, to teach us that there is more to life than physical health and strength, to encourage us to look to him for help in coping with the pressures and pains of living in a fallen world, to develop depth of character and to learn how to be sensitive and sympathetic to the needs of others.

Above all, God uses suffering to divert our attention from the present to the future and from the brevity of time to the vastness of eternity. So much of our time can be taken up with trivialities such as fashion, sport, deciding where to go on holiday, choosing which restaurant to eat in, or selecting wallpaper, but when a major disaster hits the headlines, or a serious accident or illness strikes, these things suddenly become utterly irrelevant, and we begin to think seriously about the certainty of our own death and of what might lie beyond. At this point, atheism offers nothing (literally) but dust and ashes. As Herbert Carson writes, 'To look ahead from a purely human standpoint is to see only the next hill — the continuing pain, the persistent sorrow, the debilitating illness with its relentless progress... All we can do, if that is the limit of our horizon, is to stumble on as best we can.'

The Bible gives a very different perspective and says that although God allows evil and suffering to coexist for the time being, and for purposes we can never fully understand, they will one day be eliminated and the problems they produce perfectly and permanently solved. The God who brought the present order of things into existence, and who is 'sustaining all things by his powerful word' (Hebrews 1:3), will bring this devastated and degraded world to an end and transform the entire universe into 'a new heaven and a new earth, the home of righteousness' (2 Peter 3:13), in which there will be 'no more death or mourning or crying or pain', because 'the old order of things' will have 'passed away' (Revelation 21:4).

When the atheist claims that an all-powerful God *could* overcome evil and that an all-loving God *would* do so, the person who believes in God agrees, *but adds that as it is not happening at present we can be certain that it will happen in the future.* The day is coming when God will make a cosmic moral adjustment. Perfect justice will not only be done, but will be seen to be done. The wicked will no longer prosper, the righteous will no longer suffer and the problem of evil will be fully and finally settled beyond all doubt and dispute. This is what enabled a New Testament writer to brush aside twenty years of almost unrelenting pain and pressure as 'light and momentary troubles' and to assure his fellow believers, 'Our present sufferings are not worth comparing with the glory that will be revealed in us' (Romans 8:18). *The existence of evil does not eliminate the possibility of God, but the existence of God guarantees the elimination of evil.*

This points us to two parallel truths. The first is that if we confine our thinking to time and space alone there is no way in which we can begin to get to grips with the issue of evil and suffering. Answers to questions about meaning and purpose lie outside of the 'box' in which we naturally live and think. Just as the movement of the tides makes no sense until we know about the gravitational pull of the moon, so our 'boxed-in' thinking can never find answers that will quieten our minds or satisfy our hearts.

The second truth is that the Christian response to evil and suffering *does* go beyond time and space and opens us up to wider thinking. It is rooted in a personal relationship with God, who is not an impotent spectator of human agony, but is in total and immediate control of everything that happens.

The man who was God

Yet the Bible adds an even greater truth. It tells us that God has entered intimately into the reality of human suffering and at indescribable cost has taken radical action to punish evil and eventually to destroy it. He did so in the person of Jesus Christ

In the smash-hit musical *Jesus Christ Superstar*, Mary Magdalene sings, 'He's a man, he's just a man.' She was right — and wrong! The Bible certainly makes it clear that although his character, words and actions place him head and shoulders above the sixty billion people who have ever lived, he was truly and fully human. Artists showing him with a halo or wings have got it wrong. As a child, he had to be taught to stand, walk, speak and write, and to feed and dress himself. He knew what it was to be tired, hungry and thirsty. Concerned at tragedy coming upon others, he 'wept' (Luke 19:41); on hearing good news, he was 'full of joy' (Luke 10:21). Even more significantly, he was 'tempted in every way, just as we are' (Hebrews 4:15).

Yet he was *more than a man*. Hundreds of years before he was born, prophets sent by God promised that he would one day intervene in human history by sending a great deliverer — the Messiah — who would provide the perfect answer to man's greatest need. There were over 300 of these prophecies, covering the timing and exact place of his birth, his family tree, his lifestyle, his teaching, his miraculous powers and minute details of the events surrounding his death. Even more amazingly, they said that he would be born of a virgin, something unique in human experience.

Jesus fulfilled every one of these prophecies to the letter, and in doing so endorsed the Bible's unanimous testimony that he was 'the image of the invisible God' (Colossians 1:15), and 'the fulness of the Deity ... in bodily form' (Colossians 2:9). *But why did he come?* The Bible could not be clearer. He did not come as a politician, a diplomat, an economist, a scientist, a doctor or a psychiatrist, but to deal with mankind's most radical, universal and deadly problem — what the Bible uncompromisingly calls 'sin'.

As we saw earlier, God's original verdict on creation (mankind included) was that it was 'very good', everything in it meeting with his unqualified approval. Things have changed! Today's media is clogged with reports of violence, bloodshed, racism, debauchery, immorality, dishonesty, deceit, corruption, greed and sin of every kind. A terrorist attack that slaughters 3,000 people between sunrise and noon is shocking, but should not surprise us, as the root cause of such a horrendous happening is to be found not in American foreign policy, Middle East politics or religious fanaticism, but in the depravity of the human heart, which is 'deceitful above all things and beyond cure' (Jeremiah 17:9).

The suffering Saviour

It is this horrific problem that God came to solve in the person of Jesus Christ — and in so doing he endured to the full the pain and suffering that sin causes. This has been powerfully expressed in these words, first written in the 1960s:

> At the end of time, billions of people were scattered on a great plain before God's throne. Most shrank from the brilliant light before them. But some groups near the front talked heatedly — not with cringing shame but with belligerence. 'Can God judge us?'
>
> 'How can he know about suffering?' snapped a pert young brunette. She ripped open a sleeve to reveal a tattooed number from a Nazi concentration camp. 'We endured terror ... beating ... torture ... death!'
>
> In another group a black man lowered his collar. 'What about this?' he demanded, showing an ugly rope burn. 'Lynched for no crime but being black!'
>
> In another crowd, a pregnant schoolgirl with sullen eyes. 'Why should I suffer?' she murmured. 'It wasn't my fault.'
>
> Far out across the plain were hundreds of such groups. Each had a complaint against God for the evil and suffering he had permitted in his world. How lucky God was to live in heaven where all was sweetness and light, where there was no weeping or fear, no hunger or hatred! What did God know of all that men had been forced to endure in this world? 'For God leads a pretty sheltered life,' they said.

So each of these groups sent forth their leader, chosen because he had suffered the most. A Jew, a black, a person from Hiroshima, a horribly disabled arthritic, a thalidomide child. In the centre of the plain they consulted with each other.

At last they were ready to present their case. It was rather clever. Before God could be qualified to be their Judge, he must endure what they had endured. Their verdict was that God should be sentenced to live on earth — as a man! Let him be born a Jew. Let the legitimacy of his birth be doubted. Give him a work so difficult that even his family will think him out of his mind when he tries to do it. Let him be betrayed by his closest friends. Let him face false charges, be tried by a prejudiced jury and convicted by a cowardly judge. Let him be tortured. At last, let him see what it means to be terribly alone. Then let him die in agony. Let him die so that there can be no doubt that he died. Let there be a whole host of witnesses to verify it.

As each leader announced the portion of his sentence, a loud murmur of approval went up from the throng of people assembled. When the last had finished pronouncing sentence there was a long silence. No one uttered another word. No one moved. For suddenly all knew that God had already served his sentence.

Jesus ... September 11 ... and you

As these powerful words show, the climax to God's involvement in human sin and suffering came when in an act of indescribable love Jesus allowed himself to be put to death. The Bible tells us that 'The wages of sin is death' (Romans 6:23), and that although he was absolutely sinless, 'Christ died for the ungodly' (Romans 5:6), voluntarily taking the place of sinners and in his own body and spirit bearing in full the punishment they deserved. In the Bible's words, 'Christ died for sins once for all, the righteous for the unrighteous, to bring you to God' (1 Peter 3:18).

Jesus came 'to destroy the devil's work' (1 John 3:8) and demonstrated that he had done so when three days later (again in fulfilment of prophecy) he rose from the dead, a stupendous truth confirmed by hundreds of independent eyewitness, the transformation of his followers from cowards to conquerors, the institution and growth of the Christian church and his dynamic influence in the lives of millions of people over thousands of years. Today, he offers the forgiveness of sins and a living, eternal relationship with God to all who will turn from their self-centred lives and commit themselves to him as Saviour and Lord.

Where does September 11 fit in? Jesus once reminded people of a recent catastrophe in which a tower in Jerusalem had collapsed, killing eighteen people. Ignoring speculation about the event, Jesus asked (and answered) one question about the victims and gave an unmistakable warning to his hearers: 'Do you think they were more guilty than all the others living in Jerusalem? I tell you, no! But unless you repent you too will all perish' (Luke 13:4-5).

The lessons are crystal clear. Some people have pointed to the September 11 massacre as God's judgement on the United States, but this is too harsh a verdict. We have no warrant for saying that the 3,000 who died were the worst sinners in the country, and deserved to die while others lived, or for suggesting that God is the author of sin and randomly selected them to die unjustly. We are on safer ground if we suggest that on September 11 God withdrew his hand of protection and in his infinite wisdom allowed this evil attack to succeed as a warning of the judgement that is in store for all who reject his claims.

If even this sounds too harsh, let me urge you to reflect that it is only by God's mercy that all the other people in the United States — and elsewhere — are not wiped out. The fact that 'All have sinned and fall short of the glory of God' (Romans 3:23) means that if he were to eliminate the whole of humanity in a fraction of a second neither his justice nor his righteousness would be compromised. If God were to dispense immediate and righteous judgement on us, I would not be here to write these words, nor you to read them. We are alive today only because, at least for the time being, God 'does not treat us as our sins deserve or repay us according to our iniquities' (Psalm 103:10). To put it positively, 'Because of the LORD's great love we are not consumed' (Lamentations 3:22).

When I was asked, 'Where was God when religious fanatics killed those 3,000 people in America?' I replied, 'Exactly where he was when religious fanatics killed his Son, Jesus Christ — in complete control of everything that happened.' This is the clear teaching of Scripture. Those who combined to have Jesus crucified were 'wicked men', yet his death was according to 'God's set purpose and foreknowledge' (Acts 2:23).

The second lesson is equally clear. September 11 is a wake-up call. It warns us that evil is real, that life is brief and fragile, and that death is certain. Even more loudly it tells us to prepare for a final day of reckoning when 'each of us will give an account of himself to God' (Romans 14:12) who will 'judge the world with justice' (Acts 17:31).

As 'The wicked will not inherit the kingdom of God' (1 Corinthians 6:9), we can be certain that if that judgement were to be on the basis of our own thoughts, words and actions our case would be hopeless and we would justly be condemned to spend eternity in hell, consciously enduring the appalling punishment we deserved. This is exactly what Jesus meant when he warned his hearers, 'Unless you repent, you too will all perish.'

Now comes the best news you will ever read! On the basis of the death and resurrection of Jesus in the place of sinners, God the Judge is willing to settle out of court! If you will come to him in true repentance and faith, turning from sin and trusting Jesus Christ as Saviour, *all* your sin will be forgiven, you will have peace with God and when your earthly life is over you will spend eternity in God's sinless, painless, deathless, glorious presence.

Seize the day!

The day before the terrorist outrage an American Airlines passenger noticed a stewardess breaking up ice with a wine bottle. Concerned that she might hurt herself, he asked if there was some other way of doing this. The stewardess was impressed that he should be so concerned, and after they had talked together she gladly accepted a Christian tract from him. Later in the flight she told him it was the sixth tract of this kind that she had been given recently, and asked, 'What does God want from me?' The man replied, 'Your life,' and then explained her need to get right with God through trusting Christ. Less than twenty-four hours later she was on the first plane to crash into the World Trade Centre.

As you close this booklet, let me urge you to think carefully about two things. The first is that God makes this wonderful promise: 'You will seek me and find me when you seek me with all your heart' (Jeremiah 29:13). The second is that this gracious invitation has a closing date: 'Seek the LORD *while he may be found*; call on him *while he is near*' (Isaiah 55:6). The stewardess who had the way to get right with God explained to her on 10 September had no idea that her particular closing date was a matter of hours away — and her remarkable story is a sobering reminder that nobody can afford to play fast and loose with God's patience and assume that they can respond at their own convenience.

In his perfect holiness God hates sin, yet he is 'not wanting anyone to perish, but everyone to come to repentance' (2 Peter 3:9) and in his great mercy he loves those who genuinely want to do this. Then let nothing keep you back from calling upon him here and now, asking him to forgive you and to give you grace to turn from sin and commit yourself to Jesus Christ as your own personal Saviour. Discover for yourself that 'The gift of God is eternal life in Jesus Christ our Lord'! (Romans 6:23).

This booklet is based in part on John Blanchard's book, *Is God past his sell-by date?* Contact your local Christian bookshop for a copy, or order one direct from the publisher:

Evangelical Press, Faverdale North Industrial Estate, Darlington DL3 OPH, England
(e-mail: sales@evangelicalpress.org)

If you have come to trust in God through the reading of this book, you are invited to write to John Blanchard at the publisher's address for a free copy of *Read Mark Learn*, his book of guidelines for personal Bible study.

If you need further help, please contact the following person: